PRAISE FOR RELATIONSHIP FOUNDATIONS

"As a college pastor for over seven years, I am a witness to the amplifying need for healthy relationships in the emerging generation. In an ever-expanding digitized and disembodied life experience, Gen Z is craving human connection. This is why I'm grateful for this work. It's theologically robust, clear and accessible, tactile and hands-on, and best of all - meant to be read in the context of relationships, the very thing the book is aiming to achieve."

Steve Bang Lee,
Pastor, Mariners Church

"Seven weeks. That's it. Gather your friends, your compadres, or your small group for seven weeks, and you will witness an amazing transformation—for the better—of your character and your relationships. Commit to going through *Relationship Foundations* together. Be open to God to craft or maybe re-craft your character and your relationships in areas you have thrown in the towel on and given up.

Randell artfully guides a group of friends through six weeks of reading, discussing, reflecting on biblical truths in candid, practical ways. (You need the seventh week to celebrate!)

Will it be hard? Uncomfortable? Challenging? Of course. Don't bother if you're OK with shallow and easy. But, if you really want to change, this is your opportunity. Don't let it slip by!"

Paul Tokunaga
Executive Coach and Senior Consultant,
InterVarsity Christian Fellowship

RELATIONSHIP FOUNDATIONS

Randell Turner, Ph.D.

WESTBOW
PRESS®
A DIVISION OF THOMAS NELSON
& ZONDERVAN

This book is a work of non-fiction. Unless otherwise noted, the author and the publisher make no explicit guarantees as to the accuracy of the information contained in this book and in some cases, names of people and places have been altered to protect their privacy.

WestBow Press books may be ordered through booksellers or by contacting:

WestBow Press
A Division of Thomas Nelson & Zondervan
1663 Liberty Drive
Bloomington, IN 47403
www.westbowpress.com
844-714-3454

Because of the dynamic nature of the Internet, any web addresses or links contained in this book may have changed since publication and may no longer be valid. The views expressed in this work are solely those of the author and do not necessarily reflect the views of the publisher, and the publisher hereby disclaims any responsibility for them.

Cover and Interior Image Design by Kaitlin Baker

ISBN: 978-1-6642-2241-0 (sc)
ISBN: 978-1-6642-2242-7 (e)

Library of Congress Control Number: 2021902183

Print information available on the last page.

WestBow Press rev. date: 04/27/2021

CONTENTS

ACKNOWLEDGMENTS

First and foremost, I want to thank Ash Narayan for his diligent research, his older son Connor and his college friends who became our Pilot Group, which was invaluable to the writing process. A special thanks to Jackson, James, Kyle, Mark, and Ryan for your insightful feedback and your willingness to honestly share your life experiences.

I am deeply grateful to Mariners Church in Irvine, CA that have supported our ministry. I specifically want to thank Jared Kirkwood of the Rooted Network and Mariners' College Pastor, Steve Bang Lee, to support this project.

Behind every author is an even better editor; thank you, Paul Danison, who, despite his incredibly busy semi-retirement, invested his time to improve *Relationship Foundations*.

A special thanks to Kaitlin Baker, an immensely talented artist who designed the book cover and illustration, beautifully conveys its theme.

I would also like to thank my family for your continued love and support: Hilary and Jared Furnish, Alison and Rob Amelse, Rick, and Anita Turner.

To the WestBow Press team, you are incredibly easy to work with and a true partner in this project.

Most of all, I want to thank my Lord and Savior Jesus Christ, the true Author and Foundation of my life. All glory, honor, and power be unto Him. Amen.

WELCOME TO RELATIONSHIP FOUNDATIONS

"Why are relationships so tough?"

That is the most common question I have heard after coaching and counseling hundreds of men and women on a variety of relationship issues.

Another common refrain I hear from graduates of our flagship *Rescuing the Rogue* program is: "I wish I had learned these principles on relationships when I was younger!" Whether you were raised in a loving Christian home or you lacked any real family structure, it is likely you were never taught or modeled what intimate relationships are supposed to look like. Many of you might have learned about relationships from classmates, friends, television, movies, and the internet. Hardly authoritative sources! The world is a social battleground of values, influences, temptations, and all things that are opposed to healthy and authentic relationships.

God uniquely designed men and women to be in relationship with Him and each other. We believe Jesus came to demonstrate relationship and teach us how to love well. We believe Jesus' example can inspire men and women to have healthier, deeper, and more robust relationships.

We are further guided by the wisdom of Scripture that promises if "we shall train the youth onto the right path, as they grow older, they will not depart from it" (Prov. 22:6 NIV).

This book is a seven-week guide to help you learn and apply the fundamental principles to build a healthy foundation for your most important relationships. Each week, you will engage in a variety of activities, readings, and discussion with a small group of peers. Also, you will have a few devotions and short stories to read and process on your own time. The investment of your time and attention into this program will transform your mind and heart and the way you relate to everyone in your life.

During your time together, each of you will have questions, doubts or challenges as you grow to learn more about yourself and how God uniquely designed you. Your group will be a safe place to share, and your group leader will be available to answer any questions you might have throughout the week. My hope and prayer are that you will be transformed by the journey. Let us begin to build your "relationship house" on a foundation of solid rock. Strap on your tool belt and get ready for a fun and dynamic experience.

OUR FOUNDATION
- GOD'S WORD

Throughout this book, we hope to challenge your thinking. If you are a Christian, we hope to stretch you to learn more about God and have a deeper appreciation for His wisdom on relationships. If you are not a Christian, our prayer is you will be open to not only embrace the principles covered in this book but will also explore what it would mean to have a personal relationship with Jesus.

The authority of the Christian faith is the Bible. The Bible is a collection of 66 books divided into the Old Testament (39 books) and the New Testament (27 books). The Old Testament was written at various times from about 1200 B.C. to 165 B.C. Christians wrote the New Testament books in the 1st century A.D. While the Bible is a collection of books written over a long period of time, the Bible tells one unfolding story of redemption against the backdrop of creation and humanity's fall into sin. It is a story in which Israel in the Old Testament and the Church in the New Testament both teach about God and His relation to the world. The Bible from beginning to end points to Jesus which prompted Martin Luther, the leader of the Protestant Reformation, to say you "can find Christ on every page of the Bible."

The Bible is not just a historic book. All the words in the Bible are God's words and God's Word is truth – there is no higher standard. The Bible is clear and can be understood by those who read it seeking God's help. The Bible is necessary for knowledge of the gospel, for maintaining spiritual life, and for direction in our lives. Finally, the Bible contains everything a Christian needs to trust and obey God perfectly.

While the objective of this book is not to provide a systematic theology on the subject of relationships, the Bible provides many enlightened perspectives on the subject and relationships are referenced throughout this book. Besides learning how to grow healthy long-lasting relationships in your life, we are confident that you will benefit from applying God's wisdom to every part of your life. Wherever you are in life, we are confident that the penetrating truth of God's Word will provide hope and encouragement for you now and in your future.

LEADING A RELATIONSHIP FOUNDATIONS GROUP

Leading a group study can be a challenging, but fun and rewarding experience. This book is targeted to high school and college students and young adults, so your group may be a mix of young Christians, new believers, and seekers. Each will come to the group with their own unique life story that will contribute to the group dynamic. The following are some guidelines to help everyone in your group have a great experience:

- Open each meeting in prayer and invite the Holy Spirit to guide the discussion.
- Maximize participation by directing questions to different members of the group. Invite other group members to give their opinions or share their comments based on personal experience.
- When there is a disagreement, encourage the group members to process the matter in love. Invite members from opposing sides to evaluate their opinions and consider the ideas of other members. Lead the group through scripture that addresses the topic and look for common ground.
- Close each meeting in prayer. Take prayer requests both for individual member needs as well as corporate prayer focused on specific areas of growth each member would like to see in their lives as a result of this study.

Whether you are a seasoned youth pastor or you have never led a group before, *Relationship Foundations* is simply designed to make it easy to lead a group. Each week is divided into five sections:

1. Group Activity - this is a fun and interactive exercise designed to introduce that week's subject area and allow for creative thinking. Please note that in some weeks, supplies are required, so please be prepared in advance of your weekly meeting.

2. Read Together - group members should read this material in advance of the weekly meeting. During your time together, you will lead the group through the material including having individuals read Scripture and important sections.

3. Discuss Together - you will facilitate a discussion of each of these questions emphasizing individual participation and sharing of perspectives amongst the group.

4. Reflect Together - this is a closing exercise designed to apply a specific teaching from the week's material.

5. Growing During the Week - each week there are three assignments designed to help the group members grow in their faith and practically apply the lessons in their daily lives. Each assignment should take fifteen to thirty minutes.

Thank you for your leadership. I am praying that you and your group will embrace the journey as together you learn to build strong Relationship Foundations.

UNIQUELY DESIGNED FOR RELATIONSHIP

Week 1

Group Activity

Supplies needed—fingerprint page and inkpad

1. On the page titled "My Fingerprint" in your workbook, have each person use an inkpad and impress an image of his or her thumb in the space marked.
2. Each person should spend two to three minutes reviewing the image of the thumbprint and writing down any observations.
3. Pair up with someone else in the group. Have the person impress an image of his or her thumb in the space marked and then compare each other's thumbprints. Write down what unique features and what differences you see between the two.
4. Have a group discussion about this experience.

What's Unique about Me?

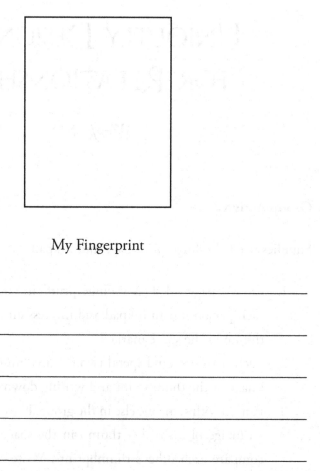

My Fingerprint

_____

_____

_____

_____

_____

What's Different about Me?

Fingerprint

There are over seven billion people on the planet and the whirls and loops of your fingerprint are yours and yours alone. You are *unique*. How awesome is that?

_____

_____

_____

_____

_____

Read Together

I'm beautiful in my way,
Cause God makes no mistakes,
I'm on the right track, baby I was born this way.
—Lady Gaga, "Born This Way"

Uniquely Designed

As God embarked on the creation of living beings on the fifth day, he did not use one organism as raw material for the next, but instead, he spoke each into existence "according to their kinds." (Gen. 1:24 NIV). All kinds of land animals were created on the same day as Adam and Eve. God created each kind of organism and equipped each with the DNA information to reproduce after its kind. That information included both the protein-coding genes and the mechanisms that regulate them to achieve dramatic differences among kinds.

Human beings were a unique creation by God. The Bible clearly distinguishes between human and beast—something evolution does not do. Even on the purely biological plane, there is a wide, unbridgeable chasm between humans and animals. Human beings have remarkable differences including a spiritual nature that other animals, including chimps, will never have. Ancestral biology cannot explain the information for physical and mental differences, much less the spiritual differences.

However, the Bible does.

Not only are humans a unique creation by God, but also each individual is wonderfully unique as you saw in our fingerprint exercise. The FBI has

4

commented on the uniqueness and reliability of fingerprint recognition. The odds of two different fingerprints matching are 1 in 10^{48} (that is a 1 with 48 zeros after it!). With over seven billion people on the planet, this means the whorls and loops of your fingerprints are yours and yours alone. Not even identical twins have the same fingerprints. King David praised God for this uniqueness when he wrote, "For you created my inmost being; you knit me together in my mother's womb. I praise you because I am fearfully and wonderfully made" (Ps. 139:13–14 NIV). Yes, you are uniquely designed from head to toe—including your fingerprints.

Image of God

In Genesis 1 God says, "Let us make man in our image, according to our likeness … So, God created man in His own image; he created him in the image of God; he created them male and female" (Gen. 1:26–27 CSB). Not only are you unique but you are also created in God's image. Being made in the image of God is what gives men and women deep value.

One meaning of being created in the image of God is that we share certain attributes with God also known as communicable attributes. God's communicable attributes are to be imitated in our lives (Eph. 5:1 ESV—"Be imitators of God, as beloved children"). These attributes include spirituality, knowledge, wisdom, truthfulness, faithfulness, goodness, love, holiness, righteousness, will, blessedness, and beauty. While God holds each of these attributes in complete perfection, we possess them in limited form. The fact that God graciously chooses to share these and other attributes with us is truly unbelievable. These attributes and many others allow us to relate to God in ways other beings cannot. The fact that we know God and are made in his image creates a personal relationship with God that is the centerpiece of the Christian life. Our identity comes from knowing who we are—image bearers of God.

Identity in Christ

What we believe about ourselves is foundational to all our hopes, dreams, and relationships. What we believe about ourselves becomes our identity. Too often people base their identities on the "measures" of the world—their job, how much money they have, their education, and material possessions. In doing so, they define themselves by those pursuits. This concept of identity is shallow, unfulfilling, and limiting. The truth is that God intends for all people to find their identity in Jesus Christ.

As a Christian, you have been adopted into God's family. The work of Jesus on the cross has made it possible for you to become one of the sons or daughters of God the Father. When we embrace our identity in Christ, we should make it the main goal of our life to learn how to know, love, and trust God as our Father (Rom. 8:15–17 NIV). God made us who we are so we could make known who he is. Our identity is for the sake of making known his identity.

When we abide in Christ, our new identity enables and encourages healthy activity. This is promised to us by Jesus in John 15:

> I am the true vine, and my Father is the gardener. He
> cuts off every branch in me that bears no fruit, while
> every branch that does bear fruit he prunes so that it
> will be even more fruitful. You are already clean because

of the word I have spoken to you. Remain in me, as I also remain in you. No branch can bear fruit by itself; it must remain in the vine. Neither can you bear fruit unless you remain in me. I am the vine; you are the branches. If you remain in me and I in you, you will bear much fruit; apart from me you can do nothing. (John 15:1–5 NIV)

In this scripture, twice Jesus promises "I am the vine." In this promise, we are transformed by a new reality in which we are empowered and commissioned as disciples. When we abide in Jesus and follow his teaching, we are promised to bear fruit in service to the world, the same way Jesus did. In fact, we are promised in John 14 that "whoever believes in me will do the works I have been doing, *and they will do even greater things than these*" (John 14:12 NIV; italics added). We will do "even greater things." How awesome is that? This is our identity in Christ.

Discuss Together

- What stood out for you in the "Read Together" section?
- What about how humans are uniquely designed impacts you the most? Why?
- How does it make you feel to know you are made in the image of God?
- Up until now, what has marked your identity? How do you introduce yourself to others?
- What would it mean for you to have a new identity in Christ?

Reflect Together

As a reminder, what we believe about ourselves is critical to developing a healthy identity. Our character is the combination of moral and ethical qualities that distinguishes one person from another. A virtue is a healthy character trait valued as being good.

1. Take one minute and write down virtues or healthy character traits you are proud of.

_____

_____

_____

_____

_____

_____

_____

_____

Did you find this exercise to be difficult? Why was it so difficult to see the good and great within you?

2. Remember that you are uniquely designed and made in the image of God. You reflect the qualities of Jesus himself.

Let's try this exercise again. This time, when assessing the virtues evident in your life, make sure you look at each and every one. If you have seen that virtue revealed in your actions or relationships *at any time during your lifetime*, place a checkmark next to it. The fact it was revealed even once means it is a part of your identity, and you have the capacity to grow and nurture this virtue.

appreciative	happy	peaceful
assertive	helpful	persevering
charitable	honest	respectful
compassionate	hospitable	responsible
confident	humble	sacrificial
considerate	humorous	self-disciplined
courageous	moral	sensitive
creative	joyful	spiritual
dependable	kind	sympathetic
determined	loving	thankful
empathetic	loyal	tolerant

enthusiastic	merciful	trustworthy
fair	modest	truthful
faithful	nurturing	understanding
focused	open	unselfish
forgiving	optimistic	wise
friendly	patient	generous

Growing during the Week

Day 1

1. From the list of virtues in the "Reflect Together" exercise, pick five virtues you believe to be the top virtues of a healthy man/woman. Of these five virtues, pick at least two that would dramatically improve your most important relationships.
2. Clearly define what each of these virtues mean to you.
3. Go through your Bible and find scripture that offers wisdom on each virtue you selected (you can use Google or a Concordance if needed).
4. Write a single statement (one or two sentences) for each virtue that describes how the virtue will impact and influence your life, relationships, hope, and future. This will become your personal virtue vision statement.

_____

_____

_____

_____

_____

Day 2

Read Scripture

> The son is the radiance of God's glory and the exact representation of his being, sustaining all things by his powerful Word. (Heb. 1:3 NIV)

For Starters

What does it mean to you that Jesus's nature is identical to God and he is bestowed with absolute power and authority?

_____

_____

_____

For Further Thought and Prayer

In the early church, Christians were faced with persecution. They were tempted to "follow the crowd" and return to Judaism, rather than continue as Christians. Write a prayer on how you can resist the temptations of the world and make Jesus the Lord of your life.

_____

_____

_____

Day 3

Read Story

When I was young, I loved baseball and passionately collected Topps trading cards of all of my favorite players. Almost all of my weekly allowance or money I earned from my newspaper delivery route was spent at the local drug store purchasing packs of cards. I fondly remember the anticipation of opening a new pack and hoping for a card of one of my favorite players like Tom Seaver or Jim Palmer.

As I began to trade cards with friends, I learned that some player's cards had more value often because of the notoriety of the player. However, on occasion, I opened a pack to find a card of an average or even below average player that had tremendous value because of production imperfections such as a miscut card, a card with a missing front or back, a card with wrong information, or even a card with a misspelled name. As my collection grew, I realized that cards of Hall of Fame players and "imperfect" cards of average players often had equally high value.

Every collectible, whether baseball cards, coins, stamps, or art has a value determined by a myriad of factors. Perfect or imperfect everything has value, nothing is priceless. Contrast this with Jesus' words in Luke 12 when he declared that man is more valuable than any animal or any other thing that God created (Luke 12:6–7 NIV). Man is God's perfect and priceless creation.

Application

Do you know how valuable you are because of "whose" name is on you?

_____

_____

_____

_____

Describe in detail your worth and value that God has uniquely and even imperfectly authored on your trading card.

_____

_____

_____

_____

For Further Thought and Prayer

Write a prayer asking God to continue to reveal your worth and value and how you can use your unique design to do His will and His work for His glory.

_____

_____

_____

_____

_____

_____

_____

_____

THE CREATOR OF
RELATIONSHIPS

Week 2

Group Activity

Supplies needed — two color Post-it notes (or colored paper)

1. On the first colored Post-it note write down five characteristics/
   qualities that are most important to you in a great relationship.
   Once finished place them all together on a wall.
2. On the other colored Post-it note write down five attributes of
   God that are most important to you. Once finished place them
   all together on a wall.
3. Everyone should spend a few minutes reviewing all the postings.
   Take notes of any things that encouraged or surprised you.
4. Have a group discussion about many of the common postings
   with each person sharing a posting.

Read Together

The first thing is this, that we must rise above the narrow confines of our individualistic concerns, with a broader concern for all humanity. —Dr. Martin Luther King, Jr.

In the Beginning

The first three words of the Bible "In the beginning" (Gen. 1:1 NIV), describes the start of a period of complete perfection. As God embarked on His creation over the next six days, there was perfect love and fellowship (perfect relationship) among the members of the Trinity: the Father, the Son, and the Holy Spirit. Perfect relationships for all of eternity.

On the sixth day God created mankind, male and female (Gen. 1:27 NIV). It is important to understand that God did not create man because He was lonely or because He needed fellowship with other persons. God did not need man for any reason. God chose to create man in His own image, and He created us for His own glory (Isa. 43:7 NIV).

After God created man on the sixth day, He said, "It is not good for the man to be alone. I will make a helper suitable for him" (Gen. 2:18 NIV). None of the animals were suitable helpers, so God made woman from man to be in relationship together. For a short time, the original perfection of relationship continued as man and woman enjoyed complete relationship with God and each other. But quickly thereafter, Adam and Eve sinned in the Garden. Shame and awkwardness followed creating a barrier between them and God. As punishment for their sin, God introduced conflict and pain into the previously harmonious relationship between Adam and Eve. Adam would lead with harshness rather than kindness and love, and Eve would desire to rebel against Adam's authority. The perfect relationships before the fall were damaged, and the introduction of sin created obstacles man would forever have to work through to have healthy relationships with God and others.

Restoration of Relationships through Christ

Jesus changed all of this as He came to redeem and restore what God intended. Christ's redemption would encourage wives not to rebel against their husband's authority and husbands to "love your wives and do not be harsh with them" (Col. 3:18–19 NIV). But there's more. The essence of Jesus is relational and through His teaching He imprinted that essential quality on all humans. The most important commandment Jesus gave us is to love God and love others (Matt. 22:34–40 NIV). Healthy relationships are so important that Jesus did not just suggest that we treat each other well, he commanded it. More importantly, Jesus set the example and is our role model of how to love people. He did everything He could to help not only his friends, but perfect strangers as well. Jesus extended His friendship and kindness to people far from God including the religious leaders and others who persecuted Him. Jesus strengthens our relationship with God as we see God most clearly through our relationship with others (Matt. 18:20 NIV). This is the unique feature of Christianity versus all other religions in that God wants a personal relationship with us, and He sent His son to help rebuild what was broken.

Relationships in Community

Culture stresses the importance of independence, but the Bible teaches *interdependence* (Rom. 12:4–5 NIV). All throughout the Bible, God emphasizes the importance of community. The book of Ecclesiastes describes the strength of community:

> Two are better than one, because they have a good return for their labor: If either of them falls down, one can help the other up. But pity anyone who falls and has no one to help them up. Also, if two lie down together, they will keep warm. But how can one keep warm alone? Though one may be overpowered, two can defend themselves. A cord of three strands is not quickly broken. (Eccles. 4:9–12 NIV)

The idea of community comes from our sense of responsibility for each other. In the Bible, God encourages us to care for each other to ensure a thriving community.

God has given men and women the grace to form multiple kinds of powerful relationships: both through friendship and marriage. The integrity of society depends on the flourishing of healthy friendships. Community does not happen if each of us is only concerned with and protecting our self-interests. God is the creator of relationships and our relationships matter. Jesus came to teach us the importance of love and how to relate well to one another. Even if you do not believe in the God of the Bible, we want to encourage you to embrace these critical principles so you can grow and nurture healthy and meaningful relationships. Open your mind and heart and see where this journey takes you.

Discuss Together

- What stood out for you in the "Read Together" section?
- How has your perspective of relationships changed knowing God is the creator and author of relationships?
- Jesus modeled being a great friend. What does being a great friend mean to you?
- As summarized in the reading, independence is often seen as a positive quality. How has your perspective of independence changed after reading the benefits of relationship and community in Ecclesiastes 4:9–12 NIV?

_____

_____

_____

_____

Reflect Together

Go back to the Post-it notes you completed at the start of this session and reflect on the importance of all of your relationships.

1. What can you do to improve your relationship with God? Be specific and think of a few small things that you can do on a daily basis.

    _____

    _____

    _____

2. What can you do to improve your most important personal relationships? Would you make a commitment to sit down with at least one of these close family members or friends and share with them the importance of the relationship and your commitment to improve the relationship?

    _____

    _____

    _____

3. If there are any damaged relationships in your life, write a
   prayer to God for His help to restore the relationship through
   forgiveness and reconciliation.

   _____

   _____

   _____

   _____

   _____

   _____

Growing during the Week

Day 1

Read Scripture

This is love: not that we loved God, but that He loved us. (1 John 4:10 NIV)

God did this so that they would seek him and perhaps reach out for him and find him, though he is not far from any one of us? (Acts 17:27 NIV)

Quick Take

What does it mean to you that God loves us even when we don't love Him?

_____

_____

_____

More to Consider

God really wants to know you better. Write out a few of your most inner thoughts and share them with God.

_____

_____

_____

Dig Deeper

Spend ten minutes writing out and sharing with God what unconditional love would look like in your most important relationships.

_____

_____

_____

_____

Day 2

Read Story

In a remote Swiss village stood a beautiful church -- Mountain Valley Cathedral. It had high pillars and magnificent stained-glass windows, but what made it special was the most beautiful pipe organ in the region. People would come from far-off lands just to hear the lovely tunes of this organ.

One day something went wrong with the pipe organ. It released the wrong tones and sounds of disharmony. Musicians and experts from around the world tried to repair it. No one could fix the problem, so they gave up.

After some time, an old man came. "Why wasn't the pipe organ used?" "It's not playing right," said the church staff. "Let me try." The staff reluctantly agreed to let the old man try his hand at it. For two days the old man worked in almost total silence. Then on the third day -- at noon – suddenly the music came. Beautiful, melodious music streamed again from this pipe organ after so many years of silence. The people in the village heard the beautiful music. They came to the church to see.

This old man was playing the organ. After he finished, one man asked, "How did you fix it? How did you manage to restore this magnificent instrument when even the world's experts could not?" The old man said, "It was I who built this organ 50 years ago. I created it, and now I have restored it."

Application

God created the universe and that includes you and me. Sin destroyed this life. It is no longer good and perfect and cannot offer beautiful music. But God sent Jesus into the world to restore it — to give us an abundant and eternal life.

Write down some specific ways that God is restoring and rebuilding you?

_____

_____

_____

_____

_____

For Further Thought & Prayer

Write a prayer asking God to continue to reveal those broken areas of your life. Pray for His continued restoration.

_____

_____

_____

_____

_____

Day 3

Read Devotional

True connections take time, commitment, and courage. While social media can make it seem like bonding is as easy as clicking a "Like" button, we're called to go deeper with each other. And that means making relationships a priority. Our seasons of life and circumstances will impact our capacity for connection, but we can all pause and ask, "What can I do to truly connect with the people I love?" Even a little bit of time or encouragement can make a big difference.

Being intertwined means choosing to stay even when it's hard. We live in a fallen world, and we are fallen people. That means inevitably conflicts will come, personalities will clash, and disappointments will happen. But we become stronger when we learn to stay because the strands of rope depend on each other. What happens to one happens to all of them. We're told, "Rejoice with those who rejoice; weep with those who weep" (Rom. 12:15 ESV). We're to share the happy and the hard of life. Community means we win together and we lose together. We cheer each other on, hold each other up, and keep Jesus at the center of it all.

Application

Who are key people who have made up your community over the years? How have these relationships strengthened you for life's trials?

_____

_____

_____

For Further Thought & Prayer

Write a prayer to God asking Him to reveal what you can do to truly connect with the people you love.

_____

_____

_____

_____

_____

RELATIONSHIP FUNDAMENTALS

Week 3

Group Activity

Supplies needed– slips of paper, pens and a hat or bag

1. Hand out the slips of paper and have each person write their name on the slip and put it in the hat or bag.
2. Have everyone draw a random slip of paper from the hat or bag, keeping the name a secret.
3. Select someone to start. They should say something descriptively nice about the person whose name they have drawn. While it should be descriptive, it should also be cryptic enough so that it is difficult for the others in the group to guess who is being discussed.
4. Everyone should try to guess who is being described.
5. The person to the right goes next. Continue until everyone has gone.
6. After everyone has gone, read the following scripture from Ephesians 4 to the group:

Be kind and compassionate to one another, forgiving each other, just as in Christ God forgave you. (Eph. 4:32 NIV)

Ask those in the group to share how it made them feel to hear the kind remarks shared about them.

Read Together

He loved us not because we are loveable, but because He is love. —C.S. Lewis

Now that you know you are uniquely designed, made in the image of God and adopted into His family, you are ready to live relationships in a whole new way. While God created relationships and designed us to be in community, He also provided us with key fundamental principles taught and modeled by Jesus that are critical to healthy intimate relationships.

Love

Love the Lord your God with all your heart and with all your soul and with all your mind. This is the first and greatest commandment. And the second is like it: Love your neighbor as yourself. All the Law and the Prophets hang on these two commandments. (Matt. 22:37–40 NIV)

Love comes from God who personifies the attribute. God's gift of unconditional love comes to man in human form through Jesus. When

Jesus was asked which was the greatest commandment as written in the above scripture, He replied "Love" (of both God and neighbor). We love because He first loved us (1 John 4:19–20 NIV). Because of this, our love for others as a Christian glorifies God.

In the English language, we only have one way to say love, so it is overused and undervalued. We love everything from various foods to cars, from movies to retailers, from people to God. Relational love is special and is best defined through the Greek word *agape. Agape* love puts others' needs before ours — it is a deep sacrificial love. This is an unconditional love that is longer, higher, wider, and deeper than our love for things of this world (see Eph. 3:18 NIV). God desires we love Him to the very heart and core of our being. A loving relationship with Christ translates to a loving relationship with others.

Communication

> When Jesus had finished saying these things, the crowds
> were amazed at his teaching, because he taught as one
> who had authority, and not as their teachers of the law.
> (Matt. 7:28–29 NIV)

Communicating well is one of the most important skills in life. It is vital to all healthy relationships. God desires communication with us through both prayer and worship. God created communication and gave great powers to words and language. As noted in Matthew 7, Jesus communicated with grace and compassion, but also with conviction and belief. The apostle Paul's instruction on communication says "Be gracious in your speech. The goal is to bring out the best in others in a conversation, not put them down or cut them out" (Col. 4:6 MSG).

Words that come out from our mouth have their source in the thoughts of our hearts. When our heart is properly focused on the Lord, in fellowship with the Father, and being led by the Spirit, our words will be gracious (always in truth), uplifting, and helpful.

To have effective communication, both parties must understand how the other feels. The hallmarks of good communication are:

1. We speak directly to the person (not through them).
2. Our message is clear.
3. We are respectful; we show care and concern for the person.

When we communicate it is important to use "I" statements and reflective listening. It is not just about communicating the content of the message, but the feelings associated with the message.

Effective listening is also a critical component of communication. We should not only hear what the other person has to say, but also listen to the emphasis and understand the meaning and emotions behind the words being conveyed. Several proverbs provide wisdom on the importance of effective listening:

Fools find no pleasure in understanding but delight in airing their own opinions. (Prov. 18:2 NIV)
Stop listening to my instruction, my son, and you will stray from the words of knowledge. (Prov. 19:27 NIV)
Like an earring of gold or an ornament of fine gold is the rebuke of a wise judge to a listening ear. (Prov. 25:12 NIV)

We are responsible for every word we say. Words can injure people as well as build them up. Words are powerful, and we need to use words wisely. "A word out of your mouth may seem of no account, but it can accomplish nearly anything – or destroy it!" (James 3:3–5 MSG). What we say is directly correlated to the condition of our heart. Luke echoed this truth when he wrote, "A good man brings good things out of the good stored up in his heart, and an evil man brings evil things out of the evil stored up in his heart. For the mouth speaks what the heart is full of" (Luke 6:45 NIV). When we abide in Christ and are filled with the Holy Spirit we communicate in a way that glorifies God. Remember, we all have a strong need for community and belonging. Effective communication is not just about speaking and listening; it is about connecting at a deeper level with another human being.

Honesty

I am the way and the truth and the life. (John 14:6 NIV)

God made honesty one of His commandments, "You shall not give false testimony against your neighbor" (Exod. 20:16 NIV). Honesty is more than just being truthful; it is about moral character. As noted above in John 14, Jesus is not only true, but Truth itself; this includes His person and character. Honesty is a direct reflection of your inner character. Your actions are a reflection on your faith and reflecting the truth in your actions is a part of being a good witness.

Honesty is mandatory for a healthy relationship. We are free to be ourselves, when we find ourselves in relationships where we can be honest. This openness allows for full and complete discussions and growth in the relationship. Honesty is about sharing the truth in a way that the other person will hear and benefit from it. Honesty needs to be tender. Truth and love are fused together. If love is not attached to honesty in our relationships, then it is not love. To have the kind of deep intimate relationships we desire, honesty must become a way of life, not just a behavior.

Trust

Whoever can be trusted with very little can also be trusted with much, and whoever is dishonest with very little will also be dishonest with much. (Luke 16:10 NIV)

Trust is the central pillar supporting any healthy relationship. Trust and honesty go hand-in-hand as Jesus taught in the above parable in Luke 16. When we are honest with one another, we build trust. It is the sense of security that allows both parties in the relationship to expose themselves fully without any judgments or fears. Trusting someone means you think he or she is reliable; you have confidence in and you feel safe with the person physically and emotionally.

There are over 350 verses in the Bible on trusting in God. It is because of our faith in God that we trust Him. He is faithful to all of His promises – He has earned our trust. In our relationships, while love and forgiveness are given freely, trust is something that is earned through actions. However, it is not an all or nothing proposition and is best illustrated by the Greek word for trust, *pisteu*. *Pisteu* expands the definition of trust from focusing on trust in facts to trust in a person or cause. *Pisteu* also contains an important endurance component – that trust develops over a period of time and not in a single moment. This expanded definition of trust helps to formulate what is commonly known as the "Five Levels of Trust in Relationships":

1. Connection – When we connect with someone we start the process of building a relationship. We have initial trust to make an investment in the process.

2. Caution – We start creating opportunities where we can observe this person's character in action and allow them to view the same in us. The process of building trust has started.

3. Consistency – When we observe consistency in honest words and actions from someone, we can begin to experience the deeper levels of relational intimacy that is only possible through trust.

4. Courage – While consistency is important, to move to the deepest levels of intimacy requires faith and courage and taking relational risks because we feel safe and secure in the relationship.

5. Commitment – Our courage to trust always leads to commitment in the relationship. The level of commitment will ultimately define the level of the relationship.

Strong trust always results in strong relationships. When trust is broken, it must be rebuilt. Building and maintaining trust in a relationship takes hard work and commitment.

Respect

So the last will be first, and the first will be last. (Matt. 20:16 NIV)

Webster's Dictionary defines respect as a feeling of admiration for someone; to hold someone in high regard and, to show consideration for someone. At its core, you respect someone you are in a relationship with even if they are different from you or if you disagree with them. You cannot have even the most basic business relationship, let alone a friendship or deeper personal relationship if you do not respect the other person or if they do not respect you. As Jesus taught in Matthew 20 above, we are all equal recipients of God's gifts, and therefore we should show respect for each other.

A secular worldview would say respect is earned. The Christian worldview demonstrates God and Jesus command respect. This is clearly illustrated through three different types of relationships.

1. Respect for Governmental Authority

God is our supreme authority, but because He ordains and establishes government, He wants us to respect people in authority (Rom. 13:1–7 NIV). The Bible also provides examples of other people in our lives whose authority we are called to respect. In Genesis chapters 39 to 41, Joseph respected his bosses even when he was a slave and then a prisoner, and he did his work as though he was working for God (see Col. 3:23–24 NIV).

2. A Child's Respect for Parents

While the Bible does not directly command us to respect our parents, the idea of respect is included in the commands to honor and obey them:

> Children, obey your parents in the Lord, for this is right. "Honor your father and mother" – which is the first commandment with a promise – so that it may go well with you and that you may enjoy long life on earth. (Eph. 6:1–3 NIV)

Jesus always respected the authority of his Father. Jesus honored and obeyed God the Father and modeled the same respect that children should show their parents.

3. Respect Between a Husband and Wife

   God's command for respect between spouses is made clear in Ephesians 5, "the wife must respect her husband" (Eph. 5:33 NIV) and in 1 Peter, "Husbands, in the same way be considerate as you live with your wives, and treat them with respect" (1 Pet. 3:7 NIV). Marriage is a gift of God who created this unique covenant relationship. When spouses show respect for one another, they bring glory to God and the church.

Discuss Together

- What stood out for you the most in the "Read Together" section?
- Why is the kind of love that God has for us, unconditional *agape* love, difficult for most people?
- How well do you listen? How can you communicate better in your most important relationships?
- Do you find it challenging to be honest and loving at the same time in your closest relationships? Why?
- With whom do you need to rebuild trust? What does that process look like for you?
- Before this lesson, did you believe respect was earned? How can you respect some of the challenging people who you need to be in a relationship with?

Reflect Together

Love, communication, honesty, trust, and respect are embedded in every one of our relationships (both good and bad). To grow healthier relationships, we need to be able identify, understand, and communicate what is working and not working. These are skills that we can practice.

1. Pair up with someone in the group (same sex if possible). Sit knee to knee across from each other. Designate someone to be Person "A," the other is Person "B."
2. Person A – take one minute to describe in detail how love and respect is reflected in one of your most important relationships
3. Person B – take thirty seconds and summarize the key points from what you heard
4. Person A – clarify or correct anything you would like
5. Person B, it's your turn – take one minute to describe in detail how love and respect is reflected in one of your most important relationships
6. Person A – take thirty seconds and summarize the key points from what you heard
7. Person B – clarify or correct anything you would like

Repeat the exercise, this time describing in detail a relationship in which honesty and trust have been challenging. If trust has been violated, try to articulate how you might be able to rebuild trust.

After the second exercise, the group should reconvene and discuss the following question:

How difficult was it to listen not just for the content of the words, but the emotions being communicated?

Growing during the Week

Day 1

Read

Do unto others as you would have them do unto you. The Golden Rule

Many people think the Golden Rule is an ancient Chinese proverb, but it was first spoken by Jesus in His *Sermon on the Mount*. A sermon which contains some of His most important teachings and which is recorded in the book of Matthew Chapters 5 to 7. The following is a modern translation of the Golden Rule:

Here is a simple, rule-of-thumb guide for behavior: Ask yourself what you want people to do for you, then grab the initiative and do it for them. (Matt. 7:12 MSG)

Application

Write down three things that you would like people to do for you. Then make a list of three important relationships in your life.

_____

_____

_____

Match up the three actions with the three people you wrote down and go out and do these things *for* them. Live out the Golden Rule.

_____

_____

_____

For Further Thought and Prayer

Journal what the experience was like. What were the most difficult and rewarding parts of this experience? How can you build this practice into your everyday life?

_____

_____

_____

_____

_____

Day 2

Read Story

I began taking my sons camping when they were very young. By the time they were seven and ten years old, they were adept at setting up our campsite, pitching our tent, and the rigors of outdoor living. They developed a healthy respect for nature and learned to be mindful of their surroundings. When we went on regular excursions during both day and night, they knew the importance of following instructions and camp safety.

One summer, we invited another family, which included my boys' "best friends" to join us on an outing. This family were novice campers, which is a kind way of saying they had no camping experience. The father went to REI and purchased the best tent, sleeping bags, and every new gadget the salesperson could think of to get them ready for this adventure.

When we arrived at our destination, all children were super excited to start swimming and fishing at the lake and all the other fun activities we had planned. However, my kids knew the protocols first to get our campsite in order. That first afternoon we had an awesome time at the lake, caught some fish that we cooked for dinner, and sang by the fire until late at night. The next morning, our friends who were unaccustomed to sleeping bags and roll-outs looked a little weary, but by the afternoon they appeared ready for a planned long hike on our favorite trails. We packed our dinner and set out on our next adventure.

After several hours on the trails, we found a nice spot for dinner and had some fried chicken and side dishes that we brought from home. The original plan was to hike back to the camp and get to bed a little earlier since our friends did not sleep well the night before, but the kids insisted on continuing our hike to a favorite spot called Sunset Ridge that had breathtaking views. Although we would not have much time at Sunset Ridge to leave enough daylight to hike home safely, I agreed to this detour.

As we got ready to leave Sunset Ridge, the sky quickly darkened as some unexpected thunder clouds rolled in. Shortly after we started our hike back to our campsite, it began to rain hard, and the wet and unpredictable terrain challenged our inexperienced camping friends. Although it was raining hard with poor visibility, I kept the entire group focused as we navigated the washed-out trail. However, the other boys kept crying out to their father, "I just want to go back home." My boys did their best to reassure their friends we would be okay, and we finally made it back to our campsite just as the storm ended.

The next morning as we were having breakfast, I overheard my friend ask my boys why they were so composed and unafraid despite the harrowing storm and challenging hike back to the campsite. My older son replied, "My dad is an experienced camper who always gets my brother and me home safely."

Application

My sons trusted me, their father, at a deep level. Most children trust their parents implicitly and with the same calm and confidence that my sons displayed. This is the same trust we should have in our heavenly Father who provides all our needs and who keeps every promise.

How can you grow this type of deep trust in your most important relationships? Write down some specific action items to help you build trust in these relationships (refer back to the "Five Levels of Trust").

_____

_____

_____

For Further Thought and Prayer

Write a prayer asking God to continue to grow your trust in Him as well as in a few specific relationships where you have struggled to trust.

_____

_____

_____

_____

_____

Day 3

Read

There have been numerous research studies done over the last few decades, and the statistics are consistently sobering: over 50 percent of first marriages and almost 80 percent of second marriages in the United

States end in divorce. These same studies reveal an even more shocking statistic: **fewer than 1 percent of couples who *pray* together daily end their marriages.** Not only do these couples not divorce; every aspect of their marital satisfaction is higher.

While prayer is how we communicate with God and how we draw closer to Him, the above statistics unequivocally demonstrate that prayer also improves our relationships with each other. The research indicates praying together increases respect and improves communication. Couples that regularly pray together agree more often on both minor and major issues. In other words, all of the relationship foundational principles we reviewed in Week 3 (Love, Communication, Honesty, Trust, and Respect) improved. For couples who pray together daily, happiness is a way of life.

While inviting God into your relationships through prayer is powerful, so is a simple blessing or affirmation. To affirm something is to confirm its truth and to strengthen it. When you bless another person, you are speaking truth into his or her life. You are calling out something you see as positive. You have the ability, opportunity, and privilege to speak a blessing each and every day into your most important relationships.

Action

For the next three days either in-person (preferred method), via telephone or text message randomly pray with, bless, or affirm the most important person in your life.

At the end of the three days, write down how you felt after each prayer, blessing, or affirmation. If you can, please ask the other person how he or she felt. Be prepared to share this with the group at your next meeting.

_____

_____

_____

_____

_____

BARRIERS TO HEALTHY RELATIONSHIPS

Week 4

Group Activity

Supplies needed - none

Present each of the following scenarios to the group and spend one to two minutes discussing their responses:

1. A group of friends is saying some pretty mean things about another friend. Some of what they're saying is true, but then sometimes those things are true of you, too. "Hey," someone says, calling your name, "you haven't said anything. What do you think? You agree with us, don't you?" What will you do?

2. You have a teacher or coach who is always getting on you for no reason, and you're tired of it. You're not a kid anymore; you deserve respect. He is coming toward you. You can tell he's angry, and you know what's coming. Right now you have to determine how you'll react. What will you do?

3. It seems that just about everywhere you look — grocery stores, convenience stores, TV, billboards — you see pictures of people

wearing revealing clothes. Some friends access Internet sites where they can see even more. One friend has figured out how to get past parental blocks on these sites and has offered to show you how. What will you do?

4. Suppose you have one test question left to answer and time is running out. You've studied hard, and you know the material, but you just can't bring that answer to mind. You could copy your neighbor's answer without the teacher knowing. Besides, you know the answer is somewhere in your brain, so it only seems fair you should get credit for it. What will you do?

After going through these scenarios with the group, ask them to reflect on the following:

- What were the factors they considered in making their decisions?
- How strongly were they influenced by their peer group in making their decisions?
- How did their faith influence their decisions?

_____

_____

_____

_____

_____

Read Together

Only those who try to resist temptation know how strong it is … A man who gives in to temptation after five minutes simply does not know what it would have been like an hour later.
—C.S. Lewis

Watch out for barriers that will hinder and undermine your efforts to develop healthy relationships. These barriers include spiritual darkness, strongholds, and unhealthy sexual behavior, all of which desensitize your emotional awareness and response to others. Although you are uniquely designed for relationships, created to be in community, and are practicing the relationship fundamentals modeled by Jesus, the enemy and the world are opposed to relationships. It is critical to understand these barriers and the tools God has given you to overcome them.

Spiritual Warfare

Whether we know it or admit it, we are engaged in a cosmic spiritual battle. This battle is described as follows:

> For we do not wrestle against flesh and blood, but against
> the rulers, against the authorities, against the cosmic
> powers over this present darkness, against the spiritual
> forces of evil in heavenly places. (Eph. 6:12 ESV)

This war is between good and bad, between righteousness and evil and between truth and lies. The enemy is real, and his purpose is to spoil all good things such as healthy intimate relationships and to deny and oppose God's glory in every way he can. God has, is and will be the victor in this battle. We must understand spiritual warfare if we are to be spiritually victorious.

In our daily lives, spiritual warfare happens in different ways; sometimes it is obvious, but most often it is subtle. The Bible says these battles occur on three different battlegrounds:

1. The World

This is the world's system of values. The world is the social battlefront where believers battle sin and evil confronting them from "without." It is a battleground of external powers, values, influences, temptations and all things that oppose God. The Bible warns against the world's values in 1 John 2:

> Do not love the world or anything in the world. If anyone loves the world, love for the Father is not in them. For everything in the world -- the lust of the flesh, the lust of the eyes and the pride of life -- comes not from the Father, but from the world. (1 John 2:15– 16 NIV)

2. The Flesh

The flesh does not refer only to sexual desire, which is part of God's good creation, but the flesh is referencing an inherent bent toward sin that every human being inherits from Adam. The flesh not only alludes to actions (sex, money, and power), but also to attitudes (lust, greed, and all kinds of selfishness). The flesh deals with the personal battleground where believers battle sin and evil "within," a battleground of internal powers, values, influences, and temptations.

3. Satan

Satan is a fallen angel, who the Bible describes as the source of evil. Satan and his allies use the world and the flesh to influence and deceive us from doing the will of God. Satan uses two effective tactics to lead us down a path of destruction. First, he deceives or tempts us. Once we have been tempted, we begin to believe the behavior "isn't so bad and it won't hurt us or others." He persists by telling us what he is tempting us to do will actually satisfy us. Second, once we have sinned, Satan piles on accusations, keeping us mired in guilt and shame. Satan is a liar, the father of lies, and through these repeated accusations he will try to convince us that we are not worthy to be called a child of God.

We cannot fight this spiritual battle without spiritual weapons. We will cover these weapons in detail in Week 5.

Strongholds

The forces of darkness described in the above spiritual battle have been given permission to temporarily occupy those areas of your soul that are not yet fully yielded to Christ. The freedom available to you in Christ is thwarted, and you are kept imprisoned by the influence of those strongholds. A stronghold is an unhealthy desire of the flesh opposed to God and His perfect will. A stronghold is a lie you have allowed to confuse and distort your thinking. Once this lie gains a foothold within your mind and emotions, it shows up in your behavior. Strongholds often destroy and, at a minimum, impair our ability to have healthy relationships.

It is important to be clear on two points about strongholds. First, a stronghold is more than sin. Satan has taken a natural desire in us and supercharged it to create something that appears beyond our control. Second, we usually keep strongholds secret and, in doing so, this continues to give Satan power. Keeping our strongholds secret is one of the enemy's most effective strategies of attack. Secrets do not keep us safe; secrets keep us sick. When you get stuck in these painful and destructive patterns of thinking, the enemy speaks even louder to you as he thrives in this unhealthy environment. You can win the battle over strongholds which we will cover in detail in Week 5.

Unhealthy Sexual Behavior

The stronghold that is most destructive to healthy relationships is unhealthy sexual behavior. Sexual immorality (pornography, lust, "sexting" and more) is sourced in the lie that that you are free to satisfy all of your desires. The negative effect of these unwanted behaviors on teens and young adults and the harmful impact on families and marriage is a significant threat to society. Both men and women alike can entertain thoughts, beliefs, and behaviors that can cross the line into what is inappropriate sexual behavior.

Pornography

The societal costs of pornography are staggering. Among adolescents, pornography hinders the development of healthy sexuality, and among adults, it distorts sexual attitudes and social realities. In families, pornography use leads to marital dissatisfaction, infidelity, separation and divorce. Galatians 5 says "you have been called to live in freedom, . . . but don't use your freedom to satisfy your sinful nature" (Gal. 5:13 NLT). "When you follow the desires of your sinful nature, the results are very clear: sexual immorality, impurity and lustful pleasures" (Gal.

5:19 NLT). The sinful nature wants to do evil. Pornography is opposed to the freedom that God has graciously granted us. The following are a few sobering statistics that illustrate the severity of the pornography crisis:

- 68% of Christian men, 15% of Christian women and 54% of church pastors view porn on a regular basis (Pure Desire Ministries 5/17/20)
- 47% of Christians report that pornography is a problem in their home (Barna Group and Covenant Eyes, 2018)
- Among young Christian adults ages 18 to 24, 76% actively search for porn (Barna Group and Covenant Eyes, 2018)
- Only 13% of self-identified Christian women say they have never watched porn – 87% of Christian women have watched porn (Barna Group and Covenant Eyes, 2018)
- 57% of pastors say porn addiction is the most damaging issue in their congregation. And 69% say porn has adversely impacted the church. (Barna Group and Covenant Eyes, 2018)

Pornography poisons you and your relationships in many different ways:

- **Pornography creates unrealistic expectations**. It shapes your opinions of what men and women should look like, and you measure love against these distorted opinions.
- **Pornography is an unhealthy coping mechanism.** A common reason cited for use of pornography is to ease boredom or stress. Pornography avoids dealing with real problems, thus weakening healthy coping skills that develop resilience. Pornography stunts your emotional maturity.
- **Pornography rewires the brain.** Use of pornography overstimulates the release of dopamine in the brain, literally

rewiring the brain to crave and demand more stimulation. Your brain and body become addicted to dopamine. And, like an addict, you do whatever it takes to get your next fix, even if it causes harm to you and your relationships.

Pornography impairs your ability and willingness to work at developing deep, meaningful intimate relationships. Pornography leaves you lonelier, not satisfied.

Being Flirtatious

Flirting is defined as behaving in a way that shows a sexual attraction for someone but is not meant to be taken seriously. When flirting happens outside a committed relationship, the line between innocent fun and intentional infidelity is blurred. Flirting doesn't only involve verbal communication, but also body language.

Flee from sexual immorality. All other sins a person commits are outside the body, but whoever sins sexually, sins against his own body. (1 Cor. 6:18 NIV)

Inappropriate Touching

No one has a right to hug or touch other people if it makes them feel uncomfortable. Unwelcome touching of a sexual nature is often disguised as friendly or paternal behavior. When the motives are improper, we are being disrespectful. We are commanded by God to show honor and respect for one another at all times (see Week 3).
Show proper respect to everyone, love the family of believers, fear God, honor the emperor. (1 Pet. 2:17 NIV)

Wandering Eyes

Wandering eyes is another disrespectful behavior that shows lack of caring and is offensive and damaging to a relationship. Wandering eyes will generally stir up envy and hurt, making a partner feel unappreciated and even threatened in the relationship. The real damage is done in your thought life. The longer you linger while looking at another man or woman, the greater the chance for fantasy thoughts to form, and the greater the risk for acting out.

Put to death what is earthly in you: sexual immorality, impurity, passion, evil desire, and covetousness, which is idolatry. (Col. 3:5 ESV)

Lust

When we allow thoughts of lust to linger, or other individual strongholds to pass the threshold of our mind, we begin to consider the possibility of acting on them or we fantasize about them. Spiritual battles are won or lost at the threshold of the mind. Once these lustful thoughts enter your mind, your emotions will reinforce the thoughts and cause defeat for most people. This is why the Apostle Paul's only solution was that you be "transformed by the renewal of your mind" (Rom. 12:2 NIV).

But I say to you that everyone who looks at a woman with lustful intent has already committed adultery with her in his heart. (Matt. 5:28 NIV)

"Sexting"

"Sexting" is obscene texting. As technology has changed, sexting has become an easier form of communication. Sexting can include sexual chat or requests for pictures or images of a sexual nature. Research has found many people experience regret or worry about the messages or pictures sent and some even report discomfort and trauma. Those who send the sexual messages or images report fewer relational benefits (emotional or sexual) and more relationship detriments associated with sexting. When these messages and images are posted through social media, they become open to the public and can have disastrous consequences on the educational and employment opportunities for teens and young adults. This practice does not show respect and honor for yourself or the other person, and it's another example of picking up hot coals and hoping to not get burned.

But each person is tempted when he is drawn away and enticed by his own evil desire. Then after desire has conceived, it gives birth to sin, and when sin is fully grown, it gives birth to death. (James 1:14-15 CSB)

Discuss Together

- What stood out for you the most in the "Read Together" section?
- What new thoughts do you have about spiritual warfare and Satan and his kingdom of darkness?
- Does one prevailing stronghold plague you? Where have you felt discouraged, defeated, and weak?
- What would it look like to have a truly transparent conversation with someone about any challenges you might have with unhealthy sexual behavior?

Reflect Together

Gather the group together and watch the following You Tube video:

The Science of Pornography Addiction (produced by Asap SCIENCE)

Following the video, discuss these questions:

1. What new information did you learn from the video?

   _____

   _____

   _____

2. Describe how pornography can rewire the brain to crave and demand more and more stimulation?

   _____

   _____

   _____

3. Since your brain has a "use it or lose it" functionality, how can you use it to acquire healthy habits?

   _____

   _____

   _____

Growing during the Week

Day 1

- Prayerfully review the list of strongholds and behaviors in the chart below. Circle the areas of your life where Satan has a foothold, or where you have allowed patterns of sin to take root. If you're not careful, this can be a discouraging exercise. Regardless of how many strongholds you circled, pick out the top one or two and start working on them now. Don't become overwhelmed with guilt or dread, but instead review them one at a time. What's important is to make an honest inventory and make a courageous start.
- Read the scripture provided to be reminded of God's truth and desire for freedom in your life.
- In Week 5, we will discuss how to break these strongholds and reclaim your freedom through the power of the Holy Spirit.

STRONGHOLD	LIES OF THE ENEMY	GOD'S TRUTH
Bitterness (Resentment, hate, unforgiveness, anger, violence, revenge)	I have power and protection when I don't forgive others.	**Forgiveness** 2 Cor. 5:17–19 NIV
Control (Manipulation, lack of trust, worry, seeking recognition)	I can control my own life	**Surrender** Matt. 16:24–25 NIV
Idolatry (Selfishness, greed, apathy, pride, stubbornness, vanity, materialism)	If I just had a little more, I would be content	**Contentment** Matt. 6:25–26 NIV

Despair (Hopelessness, self-pity, isolation, addictions, self-harm)	Even God has abandoned me	**Hope** Ps. 34:17–18 NIV
Jealousy (Spitefulness, gossip/slander, betrayal, critical/judgmental spirit)	I am entitled to all that I have	**Gratefulness** I Chron. 16:34 NIV Matt.7:9–11 NIV
Sexual immorality (Lust, seductiveness, fornication, adultery, pornography)	I am free to satisfy all of my desires	**Purity** Gal. 5:13–16; 19–21 NIV Gen. 2:22–25 NIV
False teaching & religions (Occult, Ouija board, invoking evil or dead spirits, fortune-telling, astrology, cults)	What I believe to be true is more trustworthy than God	**God's Word** John 1:1–5 NIV John 14:6–7 NIV
Insecurity (Inferiority, inadequacy, timidity, withdrawal, pleasing people/not God, lack of trust/worry, wrong relationships)	I am less than everyone else around me	**Security in Christ** Eph. 2:10 NIV Rom. 8:38–39 NIV
Rejection (Seeking acceptance, feeling unworthy, withdrawal, addictions, compulsions)	I am unlovable	**Acceptance** Ps. 139:14 NIV John 3:16 NIV
Deceit (Lying, delusions, rationalizing, wrong doctrine, misuse of Scripture)	My actions are justified if it gets me what I need	**Truthfulness** John 8:32 NIV Ps. 23:1 NIV
Fear (Phobias, compulsions, perfectionism, fear of failure)	Being afraid keeps me from harm	**God's Sovereignty** 2 Chron. 20:6 NIV Matt. 10:29–31 NIV

Pride (Controlling, boasting, belittling, taking credit, selfishness, vanity)	I am where I am because of all that I have done	Humility Matt. 16:24 NIV

Day 2

Read Scripture

> For I know that good itself does not dwell in me, that is, in my sinful nature. For I have the desire to do what is good, but I cannot carry it out. For I do not do the good I want to do, but the evil I do not want to do -- this I keep on doing. Now if I do what I do not want to do, it is no longer I who do it, but it is sin living in me that does it. (Rom. 7:18–20 NIV)

Quick Take

As discussed earlier, you have an inherent bent toward sin every human being inherits from Adam. Where do you see the "internal" battleground from *within* (lust, greed, temptation, and values) influencing your life today?

_____

_____

_____

More to Consider

Describe the inner struggle between living a spiritual life and the constant temptation of sinful desires. Write out a few of your inner thoughts and share them with God.

_____

_____

_____

Dig Deeper

Spend ten minutes writing out and sharing with God how you would like to grow closer to Him.

_____

_____

_____

_____

Day 3

Read

Flee the evil desires of youth. (2 Tim. 2:22 NIV)

Resist the devil and he will flee from you. (James 4:7 NIV)

If all you want is your own way, flirting with the world every chance you get, you end up enemies of God and his way. (James 4:4 MSG)

Quick Take

Earlier you learned the world is a battleground of external powers, values, influences, temptations, and things that oppose God.

Where do you see the "external" battleground from *without* (influence from our culture, corrupt social systems, and anything worldly that opposes God) impacting your life today?

More to Consider

What adjustments in the following areas of your life could you make to reduce your exposure to the influences and temptations of the world:

- The social media you follow (Facebook, Instagram, Twitter, etc.).

- The movies and television programs you watch.
- The websites and online content you consume.

_____

_____

_____

_____

Dig Deeper

Spend ten minutes writing out and sharing with God how you can gain the strength to resist the temptations of the world.

_____

_____

_____

_____

_____

SPIRITUAL FREEDOM FOR HEALTHY RELATIONSHIPS

Week 5

Group Activity

Supplies needed - large easel pad (or whiteboard) and markers

1. Group leader will write down the nine fruits of the Spirit on small pieces of paper and fold them and put them in a hat or bowl
2. Divide the group into two teams - A & B.
3. Team A will start and designate a person to go first as the illustrator. The illustrator will pick a paper from the hat or bowl and have five seconds to examine it.
4. The timer will start and the illustrator begins sketching clues for the team. The illustrator may not use verbal or physical communication to teammates during the round. Sketches may not include letters or numbers. The team has one minute to guess the correct answer.
5. Team B goes next and the teams will rotate and each team member will take a turn as the illustrator.

After the game is over, ask the group to reflect on the following questions:

- Which was the most difficult of the fruits of the Spirit to sketch? Why?
- How did the drawings reflect your understanding of each of the fruits of the Spirit?

Read Together

The art of war teaches us to rely not on the likelihood of the enemy's not coming, but on our own readiness to receive him; not on the chance of his not attacking, but rather on the fact that we have made our position unassailable.
—Sun Tzu, *The Art of War*

Now that you have identified the barriers of spiritual darkness, strongholds, and unhealthy sexual behavior that will undermine your efforts to develop healthy relationships, you need to understand that God has equipped you with powerful spiritual tools to overcome these barriers. You are empowered to live in freedom, transform any relationship, and meet any challenge. God will never direct you to do anything without providing the means to do it. But it will require spiritual discipline, faithfulness, and the support of others to defeat the enemy and eradicate old unhealthy thoughts and habits. When you embrace the process, you will be amazed how much your beliefs, thoughts, feelings, and actions have changed for the better. You and your relationships will begin to flourish.

Armor of God

In all three spiritual battlegrounds (the world, the flesh and Satan), the enemy has strategies and tactics to weaken and destroy us. Too many Christians lose more battles than they win and endure their walk with God rather than enjoy it because they do not recognize the enemy when they see him. They also fail to equip themselves properly for the battle. We cannot fight a spiritual battle on our own; we need spiritual weapons. God provides us with a supernatural defense by not only providing us with the Holy Spirit (we will discuss Him shortly), but also by giving us His armor to equip and protect us. Ephesians 6 calls us to "put on the full armor of God, so that you can take your stand against the devil's schemes" (Eph. 6:11 NIV). Ephesians 6:14-18 NIV describes seven different pieces of armor, each providing a different and important tool in this supernatural defense:

1. The Belt of Truth (Eph. 6:14a NIV)
    God is the source of all truth, and God's truth is absolute, eternal and unchanging. The foundation of spiritual, moral and relational truth comes from the Bible. When you follow God's Word (the Bible), you can distinguish what is true from what is untrue.

2. The Breastplate of Righteousness (Eph. 6:14b NIV)
    To be righteous means to obey God's commandments and live in a way that is honorable to Him. Righteousness is a gift from God based on Christ's work on our behalf. Being covered with the breastplate of righteousness portrays a lifestyle of trusting obedience to God.

3. The Gospel of Peace (Eph. 6:15a NIV)

   When we believe the truth of God's word and trust Him, then we have the personal, inner peace that enables us to keep our footing in the daily spiritual battle. God promises us eternal life, guidance in our daily lives, and peace in the midst of pain. Trusting in these promises answers our greatest fears.

4. The Shield of Faith (Eph. 6:16 NIV)

   The shield of faith portrays a life of protection based on faith in God's character, word, and deeds. We have to deliberately choose faith in all circumstances. We can do so not because of blind belief, but because of who God is and His promises. This is a shield that covers the believer from head to toe during spiritual warfare.

5. The Helmet of Salvation (Eph. 6:17a NIV)

   The helmet of salvation portrays a lifestyle of hope that comes from focusing on our ultimate salvation. This salvation has three dimensions: our past (we are forgiven and cleansed of our sins), our present (every day we are delivered from the power of sin), and our future (our eternal reward in heaven).

6. The Sword of the Spirit (Eph. 6:17b NIV)

   The sword of the spirit is the Word of God (i.e. the Bible) and has both offensive and defensive capacities. The sword is used defensively by applying God's word to every doubt, temptation, and discouragement hurled at us by Satan. The sword is used offensively to cause change, encourage spiritual growth through evangelism, teaching, preaching, and counseling.

7. Prayer (Eph. 6:18 NIV)

Prayer is perhaps the most crucial weapon in the spiritual battle against Satan. God is the Commander in the battle. When we connect with Him through prayer, we demonstrate our active dependence on Him and grow our relationship with Him.

Win the Battle Over Strongholds

Because a stronghold is more than sin, it is not something we can overcome on our own by trying really hard or by being really "good." This battle is fought in the spiritual realm and is beyond what we can fight without the Holy Spirit's help. Strongholds retain power unless we seek freedom through the Spirit and yield the lie of the enemy to God's truth. There are four important steps to having victory over strongholds:

1. Submission to God

We will not see victory through our own power and ability. We must submit ourselves to God. When we submit to God, we are choosing not to make things happen for ourselves. We are choosing not to control people or situations even if we can. Instead, we come under the Lord's authority, wisdom and power. The theme of submission is humility. You cannot submit to God without humility.

Humble yourselves, therefore, under God's mighty hand that he may lift you up in due time. (1 Pet. 5:6 NIV)

2. Honesty/Confession

    Next, we need to ask the Holy Spirit to reveal our sins. Once the Spirit has shown us our sins, we must confess them to God. While God knows what they are, He wants you to know them, too. Confession means "to call it as it is" or "to agree with God." This requires honesty and a real description of our behavior that does not soften the harm we have caused especially in our relationships.

    If we confess our sins, he is faithful and just and will forgive us our sins and purify us from all unrighteousness. (1 John 1:9 NIV)

3. Surrender/Repentance

    This step involves actively and aggressively turning away from these strongholds with God's help. Repentance is like saying, "I was walking in one direction, but now I deliberately turn and walk in the opposite direction." True repentance is being sorry for grieving God by the way you live. It is a desire to turn from your sins without any regrets and take a new path that pleases God.

    Repent, then, and turn to God, so that your sins may be wiped out, that times of refreshing may come from the Lord. (Acts 3:19 NIV)

4. Accountability/Freedom

    Finally, it's important to remember we can't do this alone. If it is a stronghold, by definition it will be a struggle to walk away from it. Satan will not give up ground easily. God puts people in our lives we can lean on and walk with through this turning and fleeing from sin. When we confide in a trusted Christian friend, we are relying on the body of Christ to encourage us, cheer us on, and if necessary, help us move along when the going gets tough.

Brothers and sisters, if someone is caught in a sin, you who live by the Spirit should restore that person gently. (Gal. 6:1a NIV)

The Power of the Holy Spirit

In His *Farewell Discourse* to His disciples before He ascended to Heaven (see John Chapters 13 to 17), Jesus promised He would send the Holy Spirit, the third member of the Trinity to be with them. Nine days after His ascension, in what is now known as the Pentecost, the Holy Spirit descended on Jesus's disciples. Today, when Christians make their proclamation of faith, they are indwelled with the Holy Spirit who lives inside of them. The Holy Spirit saturates us with the fruit of the Spirit which is love, joy, peace, patience, kindness, goodness, faithfulness, gentleness, and self-control. With this fruit, we are empowered to transform any relationship and meet any challenge.

The Holy Spirit abides in us and actively works within us by being our:

1. Helper, Counselor and Comforter
   But the Helper will teach you everything and will cause you to remember all that I told you. This Helper is the Holy Spirit whom the Father will send in my name. (John 14:26 NCV)

2. Advocate

   But we are hoping for something we do not have yet, and we are waiting for it patiently. Also, the Spirit helps us with our weakness. We do not know how to pray as we should. But the Spirit himself speaks to God for us, even begs God for us with deep feelings that words cannot explain. God can see what is in people's hearts. And he knows what is in the mind of the Spirit because the Spirit speaks to God for his people in the way God wants. (Rom. 8:25-27 NCV)

3. Provider

   But the fruit of the Spirit is love, joy, peace, patience, kindness, goodness, faithfulness, gentleness and self-control. Against such things, there is no law. Those who belong to Christ Jesus have crucified the flesh with its passions and desires. (Gal. 5:22-24 ESV)

4. Protector

   Finally, be strong in the Lord and in his mighty power. Put on the full armor of God, so that you can take your stand against the devil's schemes. For our struggle is not against flesh and blood, but against the rulers, against the authorities, against the powers of this dark world and against the spiritual forces of evil in the heavenly realms. Therefore, put on the full armor of God, so that when the day of evil comes, you may be able to stand your ground, and after you have done everything, to stand. (Eph. 6:10-13 NIV)

Discuss Together

- What stood out for you the most in the "Read Together" section?
- Which piece of the Armor of God do you relate to best? Why?
- How can you submit to God and turn to him and away from any pervasive sin or strongholds in your life?

As a Christian, how does it make you feel to know that the Holy Spirit lives inside of you, and is there to help, comfort, and advocate for you? If you are not a Christian, would you be interested in receiving Jesus as your Lord and Savior?

Reflect Together

As you continue to apply the principles you have learned these first five weeks, it is important to understand this is not a self-help process. To break free from harmful habits and to develop and maintain healthy relationships, you need to make yourself accountable to a trusted friend, or fellowship of men or women who will support you. Together you help each other to live lives blessed with healthy relationship that consistently line up with the values and virtues you developed in your Week 1 virtue vision statement

Accountability Partner Criteria

1. Trust
   - Accountability partners must have an extremely open and transparent relationship. This requires the highest level of confidence and confidentiality.
   - Be mindful of common social relationships that may compromise trust (e.g. related or work together).

2. Christian worldview
   - Accountability partners need to share a similar Christian worldview. This does not require advanced theological education, only that both embrace the truth of God's Word to guide their relationship.
   - If you are not yet a Christian, your accountability partner, at a minimum, needs to have values and a moral structure consistent with the principles of healthy relationships throughout this book.

3. Accessibility
   - Accountability partners should talk and meet frequently.
   - Be mindful of busy schedules when selecting an accountability partner.

As a group, reflect on and discuss the following questions:

1. Describe how an accountability partner could help you gain freedom from any unwanted behavior or unhealthy habits you have.
2. How would your relationships improve by having an accountability partner with whom you could regularly discuss any challenging issues you might have?
3. Pray about and identify at least two people who you might select to be your accountability partner and be prepared to share with the group next week.

Growing during the Week

Day 1

Read Story

During my ministry work with churches throughout the world, I have been fortunate to meet missionaries and many people who have dedicated their lives to Jesus. All were ordinary people like you and me who stepped forward in faith to pursue a call, but the story of Tom and Nancy illustrates the true cost of discipleship.

Ton ran a successful business in Northern California along with his wife, Nancy, who provided administrative support to the business. Their children were grown and spread across the country. Tom and Nancy faithfully attended and were active in their church and were intrigued one Sunday when the outreach pastor announced an upcoming trip to Cambodia. After attending an information meeting, Tom and Nancy boldly decided to join a small group on this adventure.

The mission focus of the trip was to help provide support to a local orphanage in Phnom Penh and to also help the orphanage prepare for the opening of a new school that their church had financially supported. At the end of the trip, they would travel to Angkor Wat in Northern Cambodia to visit the Buddhist temple complex, one of the top attractions in Asia. The excitement of both the mission work and visiting a "wonder of the world" carried them through the exhausting 20-hour plane trip. After a day of rest, when they arrived at the orphanage, the group was warmly greeted by the staff who were excited to have some volunteer help for several days. As the group began a brief orientation, Tom and Nancy quickly noticed something unusual, all twenty-five of the children ranging from eight to sixteen years old were girls. Soon Tom and Nancy would discover the story that would forever change their lives.

Phnom Penh, Cambodia has tragically earned the nickname of the "Human Trafficking Capital of the World." What started as the migration of young girls from rural farming communities to "work in the big city," has now evolved into one of the largest businesses in the world - a form of human slavery. Men from all over the world, but primarily Europe and China come to Phnom Penh to sexually exploit girls as young as eight years of age.

Tom and Nancy learned that the twenty-five girls in this orphanage had been deceitfully sold by their families into human trafficking and were later rescued into this orphanage. They further learned that all of these girls went through months and sometimes years of behavioral counseling to begin to repair the severe emotional and physical injuries sustained from their trauma. Finally, they began to understand that these twenty-five girls represented a fraction of the thousands of girls in Cambodia that suffered a similar fate.

Although the work was rewarding and the remainder of the trip went well, Tom and Nancy returned home emotionally drained from their experience in Cambodia. Tom regularly spent hours researching human trafficking on the internet and Nancy kept in touch with the leaders of the orphanage and school to get updates and offer prayer and encouragement. As months passed, the emotions they felt shifted between, sadness, despair, anger, and frustration. One day they received a letter from one of the girls in the orphanage describing her success with a school project and lead role in the school play and Tom and Nancy's emotions shifted to hope.

As the honestly shared with each other and prayed fervently, they made the decision that they wanted to dedicate their lives to combating the problem of human trafficking. In the months that followed, they made plans to transition their business, meet with their children and close friends, sell their home and start a Christian ministry to help address the myriad of issues around human trafficking. Finally, later that year they followed God's call and moved to Phnom Penh.

In the decade since they began their ministry work in Phnom Penh, Tom and Nancy have been arrested, jailed, sued, physically assaulted, and had young girls die in their arms. They missed the births of all of their grandchildren. They lost close friendships with several who didn't support their dramatic life change. Their decision to follow Jesus had costs.

Salvation is free, but discipleship costs everything we have. In Matthew 19, the rich young ruler wanted to enter the Kingdom of God with no costs (Matt. 19:16–30 NIV). He probably would have been a member of the average church today. But in John 6, when the great multitudes went after Jesus, He told them three times that unless they were willing to pay the price they could not be His followers.

Quick Take

Many Christians live their life to gain worldly favor. They are at peace with this world because they have sold out to it.

Have you sold out to this world? What are some injustices that you see that stir your heart?

_____

_____

_____

Application

Are you a Christian and proud of it? Are you committed to surrender your life to Him? Write a prayer to God and fully surrender to Him those things of this world that are binding you from passionately following Jesus.

_____

_____

_____

_____

More to Consider

If true discipleship "costs everything we have," as you reflect on Tom and Nancy's story, what are you willing to give up and what costs will you suffer to take the first step on your journey of being a disciple of Christ?

_____

_____

_____

_____

_____

Day 2

Read Scripture

Therefore, confess your sins to one another and pray for one another, that you may be healed. The prayer of a righteous person has great power as it is working. (James 5:16 ESV)

As it is used here, to "be healed" means to be restored. This restoration has nothing to do with your unshakeable standing with God. James is writing to Christians who have already been reconciled to God through the death of Jesus. Restoration in this context is the act of inviting others into your journey, having them pray for you, and turning away from your sinful acts (surrender and repentance).

Application

Take time to be alone and quiet and write a prayer of confession to God. While it does not have to be long, it needs to be specific and honest. Use this as an opportunity to profess and proclaim who you are in Christ, and then make a commitment to surrender and repent of anything that is displeasing to God and holding you back.

_____

_____

_____

_____

_____

More to Consider

Share your prayer of confession with your accountability partner or another Christian brother or sister whom you trust. Reflect on this exercise and how you can make it a regular part of your spiritual program.

_____

_____

_____

_____

_____

Day 3

Read

And you also were included in Christ when you heard the message of truth, the gospel of your salvation. When you believed, you were marked in him with a seal, the promised Holy Spirit, who is a deposit guaranteeing our inheritance until the redemption of those who are God's possession -- to the praise of his glory. (Eph. 1:13–14 NIV)

Quick Take

You have been sealed with the Holy Spirit. In older times, people would seal a letter by dripping hot wax on the fold and pressing a signet ring into the wax, leaving an impression. The "seal" of the Holy Spirit signifies we have been purchased by Jesus Christ. The Holy Spirit in our lives reminds us that it is finished. The presence of the Holy Spirit working in our lives is the mark of an authentic Christian.

How do you feel this seal working in your life?

_____

_____

_____

_____

_____

More to Consider

Reflect back on the game we played to open this past week's exercise on the fruits of the Holy Spirit. When you are filled with the Holy Spirit, the fruits of the Spirit will be abundant in your life.

What things can you do to be filled with the Holy Spirit?

_____

_____

_____

_____

_____

Dig Deeper

Spend ten minutes praying to God about how the Holy Spirit can continue to transform your relationships.

_____

_____

_____

_____

_____

AUTHENTIC AND INTIMATE RELATIONSHIPS

Week 6

Group Activity

Supplies needed - Bibles, paper and pens

1. Participants in the group should pair up (preferably same sex).
2. The first person (A) will ask the second person (B) to list the three biggest things he or she learned over the past five weeks: qualities about himself or herself (refer back to Week 1 virtue vision statement), his or her relationship with God and things that he or she value in his or her closest personal relationships.
3. Together A and B will each go through the Bible (using Google is permitted as well) to research a Bible verse that captures all of these qualities.
4. B will then select a single verse that will become his or her new Life Verse.

Switch and repeat the process, selecting a Life Verse for A.

Bring the group back together. Have each participant stand up and read out loud his or her Life Verse and have he or she explain what this new Life Verse means to them. After each person has read his or her Life Verse, ask he or she to reflect on the following:

- How was it having someone help him or her through the process of selecting a Life Verse?
- What process did you use to go through the various Bible verses before making your final selection?

Read Together

Mutual caring relationships require kindness and patience, tolerance, optimism, joy in each other's achievements, confidence in oneself, and the ability to give without undue thought of gain.
—Mr. Fred Rogers

Even though you are designed for relationships (Week 1), live in God's design for community (Week 2), adhere to the fundamentals (Week 3) and identify and overcome the barriers to healthy relationships (Weeks 4 and 5), if you want to experience truly authentic and intimate relationships, there is more. You need to purposely pursue intimacy intelligence. This involves an understanding of the essential characteristics of healthy intimacy, the dimensions of how healthy intimacy is expressed and received, and practical ways to develop closeness in all of your relationships.

Five Pillars of Healthy Intimacy

In his book, *To Kill a Lion, Destroying the Power of Lust from the Root*, Bruce Lengeman defines intimacy as a combination of the following key characteristics: closeness, privacy, acceptance, and openness. A further analysis adds affection to that definition and these five characteristics together provide a framework of understanding how intimacy operates in healthy relationships. These characteristics are further illustrated in the great Biblical story in the Book of Ruth which chronicles the caring relationship between a woman, Naomi, and her daughter-in-law, Ruth. In Ruth 1, one of the most beautiful passages in the Bible, Ruth demonstrates many of these characteristics of intimacy in her commitment to Naomi (Ruth 1:16–18 NIV). *Hased* is a Greek word (derived from *hesed* in the original Old Testament Hebrew) with a rich variety of meanings: kindness, love, mercy, goodness, and faithfulness. Similar to *agape*, it is an action word and involves more than feelings. It must be expressed. Ruth expresses *hased* to Naomi through her continued commitment to her mother-in-law in a great illustration of the five pillars of healthy intimacy.

1. Closeness
   Means you intentionally allow your loved one's total access to your heart. It means holding nothing back from those whom you truly trust. This type of closeness is reserved for only a very few people.

   Where you go I will go. (Ruth 1:16b NIV)

2. Privacy
   Means that you diligently protect what is shared only by the two of you. Intimacy thrives on privacy, which

is destroyed when you violate this healthy boundary. Privacy protects and builds trust.

I will do whatever you say. (Ruth 3:5 NIV)

3. Affection
Means choosing to give and receive love freely. It means your love is always unconditional and never withheld as a form of punishment or manipulation.

Your people will be my people and your God my God. (Ruth 1:16c NIV)

4. Acceptance
Means loving someone for who he or she is just as he or she is. You are not trying to change the person into who you think he or she can be. Your acceptance is unconditional, now and forever.

Return home, my daughters. Why would you come with me? ... When Naomi realized that Ruth was determined to go with her, she stopped urging her. (Ruth 1:11; 18 NIV)

5. Openness
Means intentionally being transparent and vulnerable. Your transparency and vulnerability demonstrate you trust your loved ones with your heart and your hopes.

My daughter, I must find a home for you, where you will be well provided for. (Ruth 3:1 NIV)

Healthy intimacy is all of these complementary characteristics. All five of these characteristics must be active and alive to experience healthy intimacy.

Five Expressions of Healthy Intimacy

Although you deeply desire healthy, intimate relationships, just knowing these five pillars does not make achieving them a quick and easy process. Knowledge only provides awareness. There are also five essential ways to express intimacy that when applied will begin to improve your relationships. Healthy intimacy is meant to be both expressed and received in the following ways in all of our relationships: emotionally, intellectually, spiritually, socially, and physically.

1. Emotional Intimacy
   Expressing emotion verbally or through actions that demonstrate affection.

   Examples include: sending an encouraging random text or email and mailing a handwritten letter.

2. Intellectual Intimacy
   Expressing and enjoying a mental activity together and sharing a passion for learning about a variety of topics including art, literature, science, religion, language, and culture.

   Examples include: sharing a book; taking a class together; and visiting historical or cultural places together.

3. Spiritual Intimacy

   Expressing a shared interest in religious and spiritual matters, attitudes, or beliefs. This also includes sharing a spiritual approach to life or a sense of moral beliefs one should strive to live by.

   Examples include: sharing and discussing a daily devotional; praying for each other; and going on a short-term mission trip together.

4. Social Intimacy

   Expressing affection through family, friendships, and community. Enjoying the companionship of others in an outgoing and active lifestyle.

   Examples include: hosting a small group study in your home and planning social events with friends and other couples (if married or dating).

5. Physical Intimacy (Non-Sexual)

   Note: This expression applies to married couples or couples that are dating.

   Expressing affection through the shared experience of the senses (sight, sound, smell, taste, and touch). This might include physical non-sexual contact with each other or interacting with nature.

   Examples include: holding hands and non-sexual hugs; watching the sunrise together; and trying a new cooking recipe together.

Healthy relational intimacy is not a one-way street. Healthy intimacy needs to flow back and forth, to and from each other. When your friends, family and loved ones are expressing intimacy *to you* in any of these forms, your ability to warmly receive their support and fully participate in the activity, will further transform these relationships.

Nurturing Closeness in Your Relationships

Back in Week 3 ("Growing during the Week" p. __), you were asked to affirm or pray a blessing for three consecutive days over the most important person in your life. Reflect back on how it made you feel to give this blessing and how it made the other person feel to receive these words of affirmation. You have the opportunity every day to express heartfelt intimacy by intentionally watching or looking for the good, great, and wonderful in your loved ones. Too often in our closest relationships because of a comfort in being critical, we focus on "What is wrong with you?" instead of "What is right about you?"

Ephesians 4 provides guidance for us: "Do not let any unwholesome talk come out of your mouths, but only what is help for building others up according to their needs, that it may benefit those who listen" (Eph. 4:29 NIV). Following this wisdom could radically improve all of your relationships. We are further guided by 1 Thessalonians 5, "Therefore encourage one another and build each other up, just as in fact you are doing" (1 Thess. 5:11 NIV). You can nurture closeness in your relationships through the simple practice of expressing appreciation, admiration and amazement to your loved ones.

1. Appreciation

    The Apostle Paul regularly offered up appreciation
    for his brothers and sisters in the church and his loyal
    partners in ministry.

    I always thank my God for you because of his grace
    given you in Christ Jesus. (1 Cor. 1:4 NIV)

    I thank my God every time I remember you. (Phil.
    1:3 NIV)

2. Admiration

    To express a wonder that includes approval and high
    esteem. In his final exhortation in Philippians 4, Paul
    encouraged the church to express admiration and give
    praise to each other as he modeled this by expressing
    his admiration to them for their graciousness to him.

    Finally, brothers and sisters, whatever is true, whatever
    is noble, whatever is right, whatever is pure, whatever is
    lovely, whatever is admirable -- if anything is excellent
    or praiseworthy -- think about such things. (Phil.
    4:8 NIV)

3. Amazement

    Amazement conveys awe and a joyous surprise. In
    the Bible, it was commonly used to show the effect
    of Christ's miracles, teaching and character on His
    followers. Similarly, when expressed between people,
    it is a compliment of the highest proportions. Queen
    Sheeba offered praise of amazement to King Solomon:

In wisdom and wealth you have far exceeded the report
I heard. How happy your people must be! How happy
your officials, who continually stand before you and
hear your wisdom! (1 Kings 10:7b–8 NIV)

Discuss Together

- What stood out for you in the "Read Together" section?
- Which of the five pillars of intimacy is easiest for you to apply in your relationships? Which is the most difficult? Why?
- Which expression of intimacy (emotional, intellectual, spiritual, social, or physical) is most challenging for you? Which is most natural? Why?
- In your closest relationships, how often do you find yourself focusing on "what's wrong about the other person"? How has that impacted these relationships?

Reflect Together

Pair up with another person in the group and together develop three
new and practical ways of expressing appreciation, admiration, and
amazement to one of your closest relationships. Be creative by trying
to use a combination of words, pictures, videos, events, gifts, or actions
to express healthy intimacy to the person. Use the examples below to
help you get started.

Appreciation

Thank you for running those errands for me; you made my day less challenging.

Thank you for being so flexible.

1. _____

_____

2. _____

_____

3. _____

_____

Admiration

I admire how patient you were with that teacher; he can be quite challenging to deal with.

I know you put a lot of hard work into this project, don't think that it's gone unnoticed.

1. _____

_____

2. _____

_____

3. _____

_____

Amazement

Wow! I never realized how good you are. You are truly gifted in that area.

Fantastic job! You exceeded everyone's expectations, including mine.

1. _____

_____

2. _____

_____

3. _____

_____

Growing during the Week

In preparation for your Week 7 Celebration, spend some time reflecting on how God showed up during the past six weeks. Specifically, write down the most important things you have learned about your relationship with God and your relationships with others. Be prepared to share some of these thoughts with the group next week.

_____

_____

_____

_____

_____

_____

_____

CELEBRATING NEW RELATIONSHIPS

Week 7

Make your last week of *Relationship Foundations* together a celebration. Here are three celebration elements to make it one to remember.

1. **Eat together**

   Eating together is an opportunity to connect and grow together.

2. **Share stories**

   Tell one another what you have seen God do in your life and in your heart (and the lives and hearts of your fellow group members) over the last six weeks. By doing this, you will encourage one another and glorify God. We have a final foundation illustration to help guide this discussion.

3. **Pray for one another**

   As you get ready to close this chapter of your group time together, lift one another up to God thanking Him for what He has done and inviting Him into the next phase of each other's lives.

Prayer requests by your group members:

_____

_____

_____

_____

_____

_____

Your New Foundation

Relationships are one of the most valuable treasures, if not the most valuable, we have on Earth.

Why do relationships matter so much? Because God is a God of relationships. God did this because He simply wants a growing and flourishing relationship with us. God lives and breathes relationships. His perfect relationship within Himself, the Trinity, shows how much God values relationships, and how He wants us to live in community and flourish in our relationships with one another.

As we experience the overwhelming love of Christ, it compels us to share that love with others. Colossians 3 says, "And above all these put on love, which binds everything together in perfect harmony" (Col. 3:14 NIV). So whether that's your relationship with your spouse, children, church community, co-workers, or even neighbors, when we are fully united with God through Christ, it causes us to be overfilled with love and pour into these relationships.

Over the past six weeks, you have been on an adventure to experience through your group, the foundation for healthy intimate relationships. Foundations are often unseen and taken for granted, but they provide stability for what rests on them. When building a house, there is design and planning required well in advance of the first shovel of dirt being removed. A carefully designed and well-built foundation not only ensures a house will provide adequate shelter, but also one that will stand strong when a storm or even a natural disaster strikes. The blueprint of the relationship foundation you have learned was designed by God. A house foundation and relationship foundation are similar. Let's take a look.

A Solid Foundation

Therefore everyone who hears these words of mine and puts them into practice is like a wise man who built his house on the rock. The rain came down, the streams rose, and the winds blew and beat against that house; yet it did not fall, because it had its foundation on the rock. But everyone who hears these words of mine and does not put them into practice is like a foolish man who built his house on sand. The rain came down, the streams rose, and the winds blew and beat against that house, and it fell with a great crash. (Matt. 7:24-27 NIV)

Weeks 1 & 2
Site Selection / Preparing the Soil
Uniquely Designed for Relationship by God

Week 3
The Foundation / Footings
Relationship Fundamentals

Week 4
Outside Forces/Inside Poor Materials
Barriers to Healthy Relationships

Week 5
Erecting the Outer Walls and Weatherproofing
Spiritual Freedom for Healthy Relationships

Week 6
Finishing the Inside of the Home
Expressing Healthy Intimacy

Key components of the picture illustration:

Weeks 1 & 2: Site Selection and Preparing the Soil (*Designed for Relationship by God*)

Real estate developers will tell you site selection is critical. They search for the best place to build, not on sand, but on solid ground. The soil must be properly graded and compacted to be properly prepared to build the foundation.

You are uniquely designed and made in the image of God. He selected you as the "perfect site" for a relationship not only with Him, but in community with others. Your identity is in Christ, and He prunes and prepares you for relationship.

Week 3 - The Foundation/Footings (*Relationship Fundamentals*)

The footings need to be engineered and dug to a proper depth. A solid foundation transfers the load from the structure to the ground allowing the structure to withstand most anything.

God provided you with key fundamental principles taught and modeled by Jesus that are critical to healthy intimate relationships: love, communication, honesty, trust, and respect. When these principles are in solid footings, during difficult times the load can be transferred from the relationship to the solid ground of God.

Week 4 - Outside Forces/Inside Poor Materials (*Barriers to Healthy Relationships*)

Even with a great site, properly prepared soil, and well-engineered footings, there are outside forces that can compromise the foundation. These forces can originate from the world (weather) or from within (substandard materials).

The enemy and the world create barriers to hinder and undermine our efforts to develop healthy relationships. These barriers include spiritual darkness, strongholds, and unhealthy sexual behavior.

Week 5 - Erecting the Outer Walls and Weatherproofing (*Spiritual Freedom for Healthy Relationships*)

The footings need to be sealed. The sealant acts as a shield and moisture barrier. After the footings are cured and sealed, the outer walls are constructed starting with a block wall in a corner section of the foundation. Masons use "leads" to construct accurately flat and upright walls that complete the foundation of the home.

God has equipped us with powerful spiritual tools to overcome the barriers to healthy relationships. Through the Holy Spirit, we have an advocate, protector, and provider (a sealant) who equips us with spiritual tools like the Armor of God to gain true freedom.

Week 6 - Finishing the Inside of the Home (*Expressing Healthy Intimacy*)

After the foundation is complete, you are now able to work on the inside of the home. Installing flooring, paint, kitchen appliances and other fixtures that are necessary to complete your home. You are now ready to live in your home.

By purposely pursuing intimacy intelligence and practical ways to express and receive intimacy, you can begin to develop closeness in your relationships. You now have a solid foundation for all of your relationships to flourish.

Moving Forward

The relationships you will build on this foundation will not only be durable, but with your continued investment and partnership with Jesus and the Spirit, will weather the storms of life. All relationships need care and attention for them to grow into something healthy and long-lasting. When the storms of life hit (and they will), this strong foundation built on the solid ground of God and the web of strength in these carefully designed components, will not only withstand the forces, but will also endure and prosper. As you grow healthy and authentic intimacy in your relationships, your home reflects the character of God and love of Jesus. You might remodel or even add a second story to some relationships. As long as you keep the front doors open for Jesus to be in the center of your relationships, you will enjoy intimate relationships that will last.

Final Reflections

As you celebrate with your group the completion of *Relationship Foundations*, reflect on the following:

- In the opening Week 2 "Group Activity," you wrote down five characteristics/qualities that are most important to you in a great relationship. Reflect back on that exercise and discuss with the group how you can now live those out in your relationships today.
- Share with the group any differences you see in yourself over the past seven weeks. Share how you see God working in your life.
- Share with the group how your new relationship foundation is going to restore or strengthen your most important relationships.
- As you close, have each person pray for another person in the group.

_____

_____

_____

_____

_____

_____

SOURCES AND REFERENCES

Week 1 - Uniquely Designed for Relationship

Gaga, Lady. "Born this Way." Accessed October 19, 2020. http://www.lyrics.com/lyric/23051878/Lady+Gaga/Born+This+Way.

Proceedings of the National Academy of Sciences of the United States of America (PNAS), *Accuracy and Reliability of Forensic Latent Fingerprint Decisions* by Bradford T. Ulery, R. Austin Hicklin, JoAnn Buscaglia, and Maria Antonia Roberts, May 10, 2011. Accessed October 19, 2020. https://www.pnas.org/content/108/19/7733.

Turner, Randell, *Rescuing the Rogue*, Watertown, WI: TFW International 2012

Week 2 - The Creator of Relationships

King, Martin Luther. "The Birth of a New Age." Speech, Alpha Phi Alpha Fraternity, Buffalo, NY, August 11, 1956.

Lucado, Max. *Six Hours One Friday: Living the Power of the Cross.* Nashville: Thomas Nelson, 2004.

Stine, Crystal. *Craving Connections: 30 Challenges for Real-Life Engagement*. Nashville: B & H Publishing, 2017.

Week 3 - Relationship Fundamentals

Lewis, C.S. *The Problem of Pain*. San Francisco: Harper Collins, 2001.

Nissley, Ronda. "An Amazing Secret of Marriage Success." Accessed October 19, 2020. https://www.encompasscc.org/blog/an-amazing-secret-to-marriage-success.

Week 4 - Barriers to Healthy Relationships

Lewis, C.S. *Mere Christianity*. San Francisco: Harper Collins, 2001.

The Science of Pornography Addiction. Accessed October 19, 2020. http://www.youtube.com/watch?v=1Ya67aLaaCc.

Mariners Church. *Rooted*. Irvine, CA: 2011.

Turner, Randell. *Rescuing the Rogue*. Watertown, WI: TFW International, 2012.

Week 5 - Spiritual Freedom for Healthy Relationships

Tzu, Sun. *The Art of War*. Translated by Thomas Cleary. Boston: Shambhala Publications, 1988.

Turner, Randell. *Rescuing the Rogue*. Watertown, WI: TFW International, 2012.

Week 6 - Authentic and Intimate Relationships

Lengeman, Bruce. *To Kill a Lion*. Apopka, FL: Certa Books, 2010.

Turner, Randell. *Rescuing the Rogue*. Watertown, WI: TFW International, 2012.

Week 7 - Celebrating New Relationships

Baker, Kaitlin. *Illustration of House Foundation*. 2020.

ABOUT THE AUTHOR

Randell Turner, Ph.D., is an author, a counselor, and a pioneer in the men's and fatherhood movement. He has developed award-winning resources for the National Center for Fathering, the National Fatherhood Initiative, Prison Fellowship, and Fatherhood.gov. Specializing in healthy masculine intimacy, he has dedicated over 20 years to working with men who feel broken, rejected, isolated, and lonely because of their "intimacy ignorance." His personal and professional experience inspired the creation of *Rescuing the Rogue*, a study that equips men to forge intimate relationships that last a lifetime.

The passion and purpose of that inspires his writing, workshops and coaching is to enable men and women to courageously develop authentically intimate relationships grounded by a deeply devoted God-given and God-guided love with family and friends.

Most importantly, Randell is father of two and grateful grandfather of seven gorgeous grandchildren.

Printed in the United States
by Baker & Taylor Publisher Services